CH

D0744150

EXPLORE
ANCIENT
WORLDS

THE
BYZANTINE
EMPIRE

MARY BOONE

Mitchell Lane
PUBLISHERS
P.O. Box 196
Hockessin, Delaware 19707
Visit us on the web: www.mitchelllane.com
Comments? email us: contactus@mitchelllane.com

EXPLORE
ANCIENT
WORLDS

Ancient Assyria • Ancient Athens
The Aztecs • Ancient Babylon
The Byzantine Empire • The Celts of the British Isles
Ancient China • Ancient Egypt
Ancient India/Maurya Empire • Ancient Sparta

ABOUT THE AUTHOR: Mary Boone has written
more than two dozen books for young readers,
including biographies about musicians Pink
and 50 Cent, and sports stars Tim Lincecum
and Sue Bird. She, her husband Mitch, and
their kids, Eve and Eli, live in Tacoma, Wash.

PUBLISHER'S NOTE: The facts on which the story
in this book is based have been thoroughly
researched. Documentation of such research
can be found on page 45. While every possible
effort has been made to ensure accuracy, the
publisher will not assume liability for damages
caused by inaccuracies in the data, and
makes no warranty on the accuracy of the
information contained herein..

Printing 1 2 3 4 5 6 7 8 9

**Library of Congress
Cataloging-in-Publication Data to come**

eBook ISBN: 9781612283562

PLB

CONTENTS

A view of Constantinople from the neighboring city of Pera.

Birth of an Empire

The story of the Byzantine Empire is filled with tales of bloody struggle and ruthless warlords. The Empire's existence was marked by religious devotion, political deception, brutal attacks, impressive artwork, and a sophisticated economic system. Its heroes and villains seem like the sort of characters you'd see in a movie—but they were very real.

The Byzantine Empire began in A.D. 330, when Emperor Constantine I made the city of Byzantium the capital of the Roman Empire. The city had been established by Greek settlers about 1,000 years earlier. It was located on a peninsula tucked in between the Black and Aegean Seas and was a popular travel route for merchants. The fact that they could get to it by land or by sea made it a particularly good location for a city, and it became a crossroads of trade between Europe and Asia.

Constantine launched a massive building program in an effort to establish many of the same kinds of public monuments that Rome had had for several centuries and thereby make it fitting as the capital of the Empire. The project took six years and the buildings included many religious monuments honoring Christianity. Constantine brought artwork and sculptures from all parts of the empire to decorate his new city. The Serpent Column from Greece, an Egyptian obelisk, and statues representing pagan gods and heroic leaders were all put on display.[1] Some of the city's

Distances to the important cities of the empire were inscribed on Constantinople's Milion Stone. Today, remains of the Milion Stone are located near the water tower in the Sultanahmet district of Istanbul, Turkey.

most important treasures were brought directly from the Holy Land by Constantine's mother.

One of the city's focal points was a dome supported by four arches. The structure was called the Milion, or milestone, and became the point from which all distances in the empire were measured.

When the construction was completed, a huge celebration was held. Citizens attended horse and chariot races, banquets were held, clothing was given to residents, and elaborately decorated public baths were reopened.[2] At first the new city was called "Second Rome" but the name was soon changed to Constantinople, in honor of Constantine.

At the time, Rome was a city teetering on the brink of war. Many citizens thought the emperor had too much power while others simply wanted a new leader. Some scholars think that Constantine wanted out of Rome for his own safety; others believe Rome's location was too remote to be effective. Whatever the reasons, almost as soon as the city of Constantinople was completed, Constantine decided to make it the new imperial capital. As Constantinople's importance grew, so did its population. Within 200 years of its founding, the city is thought to have had nearly 500,000 residents.[3]

While Constantinople prospered, Rome's population was shrinking. Its buildings were beginning to fall apart because there wasn't enough money to maintain them.

This bust commemorates Emperor Constantine I, also known as Constantine the Great. He is remembered for being the first Roman emperor to convert to Christianity and is considered the founder of the Eastern Roman Empire.

The Roman Empire was divided into two halves, as shown on this map. The Eastern Empire was also referred to as Pars Orientis; the Western Empire was also known as Pars Occidentalis.

Even with a new capital, the Roman Empire was huge—stretching nearly 2,500 miles from the Atlantic Ocean to the Persian Gulf (approximately the distance between New York City and Los Angeles). Governing such an enormous territory was difficult so, in 364, Emperor Valentinian I divided the Empire into two halves—East and West—with two separate rulers. Christianity was the official religion of both parts of the empire, though in the East the emperors were considered heads of the church as well as heads of state. In the West, the pope was the ultimate authority.

Officially, the two parts of the empire were viewed as a single state. In reality, there were many differences between the two halves.

The Western Empire kept the name of Rome and was ruled over by Emperor Valentinian I from Milan. The Eastern Empire eventually took the name Byzantium from the original name of the city where

Constantinople now stood. The Byzantine Empire covered the land that is now occupied by Greece, the Balkan Peninsula, Turkey, Syria, and Egypt.

The split was especially difficult for the western part of the empire because it had fewer residents and less money than its eastern counterpart. In 376, more than 60,000 Germanic immigrants known as Visigoths were given permission to settle in the Eastern Empire. Eastern officials reportedly stole from the new settlers, made their children slaves, and tried to kill their leader. The Visigoths became a vicious army that retaliated by killing Valens, the Eastern emperor. They eventually made a deal with the Western emperor, who allowed the Visigoths to settle there. In the end, the Visigoths became upset with Western Empire officials and they captured Rome in 410. Led by Alaric, the ragtag Visigoth army looted and pillaged Rome for three long days.

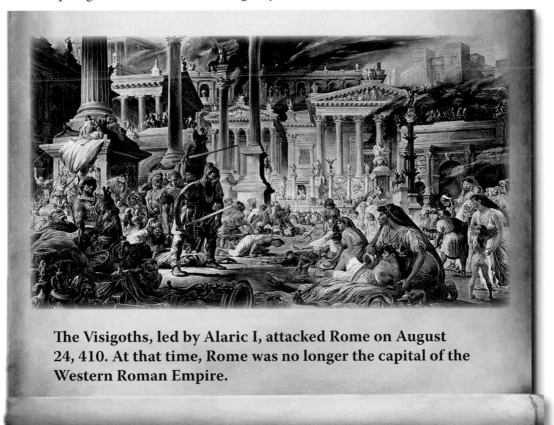

The Visigoths, led by Alaric I, attacked Rome on August 24, 410. At that time, Rome was no longer the capital of the Western Roman Empire.

The walls of Constantinople were the most famous of the medieval world. They were made primarily of mortared rubble, faced with blocks of limestone and reinforced by layered red brick.

Residents of the Byzantine Empire were shocked by the capture of Rome. The news brought more than 16,000 volunteers to Constantinople to build a series of massive walls to protect their city.[4]

The walls of Constantinople were the most famous of the medieval world.[5] The city was encased in a circuit of 14 miles of walls, reinforced by more than 400 towers and bastions, and several strong points and fortresses. Built from mortared rubble, limestone and red brick, two separate walls—one inside the other—wrapped around Constantinople like a series of belts. Even if an enemy army made its way through the first wall, the second stood ready to protect the city. The walls were 30 to 60 feet high and included a series of moats, which provided even more protection. The remains of several of the walls still stand today.

Baths of Zeuxippos

Roman bath

Construction of the Baths of Zeuxippos began in the time of old Byzantium and was finished by Constantine the Great. They were named after the god Zeus because they were built on a site where a temple honoring him had previously stood.

Constantine made the baths into a real showplace, decorating them with marble, bronze, mosaics and a huge collection of statues honoring historic figures, gods and mythological heroes. Other public bath houses were built during these times, but the Baths of Zeuxippos were famous for their extravagance and were among the most popular.

As fancy as they were, the baths were designed for public bathing. For a small fee, members of the general public could bath or exercise there. Attendants were employed to oversee the baths and enforce rules. Men and women, for example, were not allowed to bathe together. They could either be in separate baths, or bathe at different times of the day. Many of the public baths featured a progression of chambers, from cold to very hot.

Fire destroyed the Baths of Zeuxippos and many surrounding buildings in 532. The baths were reconstructed soon afterward, though the practice of public bathing eventually declined. During the eighth century, parts of the building became a prison known as Noumera, while another part became a silk factory.

The Baths of Zeuxippos have all but disappeared today. In 1927 and 1928, archeologists discovered several statue bases and an extremely damaged statue head from the baths. The excavation was important because it was the first time historians had been able to identify a type of Byzantine glazed pottery called Zeuxippos Ware, made during the time of Constantine.

Byzantine emperors refused to be considered "kings." Instead, they argued, they were chosen by God and worked within the assistance of a senate, consuls and magistrates.

CHAPTER 2

A Complex Machine

Many layers of government and thousands of complicated rules governed Byzantine society. For the most part, both the Empire's social structure and political system were based on Rome's, with a ruler known as the emperor at the top.

The Byzantine emperor was thought to be chosen by God and was head of the church as well as head of state. He appointed church bishops and passed both religious and secular laws. He called together councils, directed their discussions, and enforced their decisions. He made it his number-one priority to defend the church and to share his faith with others. No one could override his rulings and citizens didn't get to vote on them. The emperor alone had the power to establish taxes, declare wars, and name cities.

One of the Byzantine emperor's major responsibilities was taking part in the region's official ceremonies, festivals, state banquets, and religious events. Guests at these official events were assigned titles that indicated where they could sit in relation to the emperor, to whom they could talk, and even the topics they were allowed to discuss. The rules and rituals governing interactions with the emperor eventually became so complicated that entire books were written to help explain proper political etiquette.[1]

Of course, even an emperor could use a little help, so a cabinet of advisors called the *sacrum consistorium* met regularly to provide advice and guidance. Additionally, the Byzantine senate worked to propose legislation, though it didn't have the power to pass this legislation. Many government officials worked throughout the region to carry out the emperor's orders.

Kings were born into their positions; emperors were not. Emperors did have the power to appoint their own successors and most chose a son, though an occasional trusted friend was selected. If the heir was not the emperor's son, he often adopted him so that his dynasty would continue. Eventually the empire would have 16 different dynasties, along with five brief periods when there was no dynasty.

An emperor generally waited until later in life to select his heir. Once a successor was named, he would begin to serve as co-ruler, learning his duties on the job.

Even though the emperor was very powerful, his heir could not be crowned until there had been a formal vote by three groups: the senate, the army, and citizens of the empire. On the occasions when an incompetent ruler got into office, these same three groups had the power to vote him out.[2] Sometimes, a vote became unnecessary because a revolt broke out to overthrow the emperor. Over the years, some emperors were killed, thrown in prison or blinded—a disability which, according to Byzantine law, made them unable to rule.

There could only be one emperor at a time, with the exception of the short time period when a successor was serving as co-ruler. Women who were related to the emperor could serve as empresses and there could be several of them serving at the same time. For example, Pulcheria, sister of Emperor Theodosius II, served as empress at the same time as his wife, Aelia Eudocia, though the relationship between the two women was strained.

Theodora, wife of Emperor Justinian I, was among the empire's most popular empresses and—some historians suggest—may have been the most powerful woman in Byzantine history. Theodora was the daughter of a bearkeeper at Constantinople's hippodrome, and Justinian was attracted

Empress Theodora is thought to have been the most influential woman in the Byzantine Empire's history.

to both her beauty and intelligence. She provided political advice to her husband, greeted foreign guests, and presided over government festivals. Her name is mentioned in nearly all the laws passed during that period and she is remembered as one of the first rulers to recognize the rights of women, passing laws to protect young girls from being sold into slavery and changing divorce laws to give greater benefits to women. One of the greatest illustrations of her influence came in the Nika revolt of 532. Constantinople's political factions united in their opposition to the government and appointed a rival emperor. Justinian's advisers urged him to flee, but Theodora encouraged him to stay and save his empire. He did and the rioters were ultimately rounded up and put to death.[3]

With government controlling most aspects of Byzantine life, it should come as no surprise that it also regulated the prices of food and other commodities. Revenue from trade made up a small portion of the empire's budget; a much larger percentage came from taxes on people and products. The empire's wealthiest citizens viewed those who farmed the land and manufactured goods as the lowest members of society. Those with money owned the land, but left the work of producing goods to commoners; those peasants provided most of the empire's tax revenues.

The army was the primary military body of the Byzantine armed forces.

The Byzantines' philosophy regarding trade was traditional and straightforward: Anything that might aid the enemy should never leave the empire. Aside from the obvious weapons and ammunitions, the list of prohibited items included purple silk (which was reserved for the imperial family), precious metals, candles, soap and fish.[4]

The military played an important role in the Byzantine government. By 565, the Byzantine army is thought to have had 150,000 members.[5] A much smaller but still powerful navy also worked to defend the empire. Byzantine rulers recruited troops by offering them land in return for their military service. The land could not be sold, but it could be passed from generation to generation, in exchange for continued military service. Many immigrants were recruited for the army in this manner.

As prepared as they were to go to war, the Byzantines preferred negotiation over battle. Government officials worked tirelessly to try to establish good relations with other states. The sons of foreign leaders were often invited to attend Constantinople's outstanding schools and, on more than one occasion, an emperor married a princess from another land if he thought the marriage would help smooth relations with that state. German emperor Otto II, for example, married Byzantine princess Theophano in 972, forging an alliance between the German imperial family and the Byzantine aristocracy.[6]

Byzantine Social Classes

The Byzantine Empire was made up of three distinct social classes.

The first of the three—at the top of the ladder—was the aristocratic class. Government officials, top military officers, wealthy merchants, and large landowners were all members of the upper class. The wealthiest members of Byzantine society wore fine clothing, attended extravagant banquets, had staffs of servants, and many maintained both city and country homes.

Byzantine clothing

The middle class was made up of medium-sized landowners, merchants, and industrialists. Members generally lived in cities and, while they didn't live as well as those in the aristocracy, most could afford to have a servant or two.

The third class—lowest in the hierarchy—was often referred to as the peasant class. They worked hard, long hours on public works projects, building canals and channels, repairing roads and maintaining parks. In exchange for their labor, the government provided food, shelters, orphanage services and basic healthcare. Other members of the peasant class lived in the country, providing farm labor on large settlements in exchange for food and a place to sleep. The peasant class was the largest in Byzantine society.

The clergy—priests, bishops, monks and nuns—did not form a distinct class within the Byzantine society though they enjoyed certain special privileges. They existed in all social levels.

Slavery did exist in Byzantium. Some slaves were privately owned while others belonged to the state. Byzantines' beliefs prohibited them from keeping Christians as slaves, so only non-Christians were enslaved.

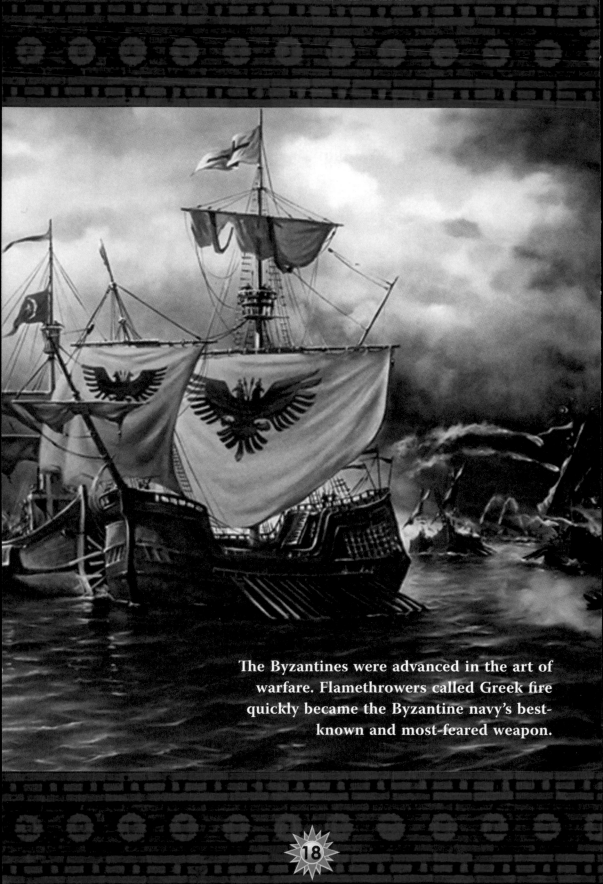

The Byzantines were advanced in the art of warfare. Flamethrowers called Greek fire quickly became the Byzantine navy's best-known and most-feared weapon.

Battles, Battles Everywhere

Almost from the beginning, the Byzantine Empire had political enemies. Other states, nomadic tribes, and barbarians living near the empire were hungry for power. Byzantium's rich culture and many art treasures made it a very tempting target.

Early on, the Empire's army was forced to fight off persistent attacks by Persian and Muslim invaders. Constantinople's location—with water on three sides and a strong wall on the fourth—was fairly secure and initially helped keep the city safe from attack.

Some of the Empire's most notable battles came under the reign of Emperor Justinian I, who ruled from 527 to 565. Justinian was a capable leader who wanted his empire to be strong and his people to be happy. He ruled with the help of his wife, Empress Theodora.

In an effort to expand Byzantium's boundaries, Justinian's armies—often under the leadership of Belisarius, one of the empire's best generals—were almost always at war. These wars cost an enormous amount of money, leaving the Empire nearly bankrupt. Additionally, soldiers were scattered all over the now-larger nation, making Byzantium an easy target for states eager to attack.

Beginning in the 550s, a group of barbarians known as Slavs began raiding the Empire's Balkan territories. Byzantine military officials came up with a clever plan to stop the Slavs. They negotiated with the Avars, an especially warlike tribe, to attack the Slavs. The Empire figured if the Slavs were fighting the Avars, they'd be too busy to invade the Balkans and nearby cities.

Part of the plan worked. The Avars were able to overcome the Slavs. However, in an effort to escape the Avars, thousands of Slavs fled even deeper into the Balkans and established settlements. The Slavs refused to abide by Byzantine law, thus creating ongoing problems for their new rulers.

Byzantine soldiers were trained to fight with swords and, as time wore on, archery was extensively practiced.

In 582, the Avars turned on the Byzantines and began raiding the Balkans themselves. The twist was that, by this time, the Avars' armies included Slavs, whom the Byzantines had originally hired the Avars to conquer.

Maurice became emperor of Byzantium in 582. He was honest, well-educated, and an experienced military man, but he faced multiple urgent threats. He was forced to send troops to several different areas: Persia, the Balkans, and Italy.

As these conflicts continued, the empire's financial situation became bleaker. In 588 Maurice cut the pay of his soldiers by 25 percent. Upset by this threat to their income, the men threw out their commander and chose a new leader. This new leader restored order, defeated an invading Persian army, and convinced the emperor to restore the army's pay.

Maurice was victorious in the Persian War but his troops got little reprieve. Battles continued in the Balkans, where his soldiers were able to successfully fight off the Slavs.

Still concerned with finances, Maurice ordered the soldiers to stay in the countryside throughout the winter of 593, living off what little they could find there. The troops were upset by this order and left their posts for safer, more pleasant quarters many miles away. With the troops gone from the country, the Slavs were once again able to move into Byzantine territory.[1]

Slowly the Byzantines pushed the Slavs back. But in 602, Maurice once again tried to save money and ordered his army to spend the winter in the field in harsh conditions. He even wanted them to launch a new series of attacks. For the army, that was the last straw. Led by an officer named Phocas, they marched back to Constantinople and overthrew Maurice. Phocas became the new emperor. Maurice and his family were executed in the uprising. He was the first Byzantine emperor to die as the result of a revolt.[2]

While empire officials were distracted by the revolt, the Persians began attacking the Byzantine Empire again. The Empire's army was weak and this time the Persians were able to conquer the lands occupied today by Syria, Palestine, Israel, and Egypt.

The Emperor Heraclius, who ruled from 610 to 640, spent 10 years revitalizing the Byzantine economy and rebuilding its army. With well-armed and reorganized troops, he was able to conduct several successful military campaigns during which he defeated the Persians and regained the areas they had previously taken.

Just as the Byzantines were beginning to feel secure, they were confronted with a new enemy. In 634 Arabs, who were newly converted to the Islamic faith, attacked the Byzantine Empire. Within a few years they had conquered Palestine, Syria, Persia, Egypt and much of North Africa.

Nearly every year, Arab troops also attacked the border between the Byzantine Empire and their own lands. Several times they even tried to assault Constantinople itself. The constant struggle weakened the empire.

Persian soldiers besieged the Byzantine city of Amida in 502. The Byzantines were able to repel the assault for three months before Persia claimed victory.

It was also threatened by the Bulgars who, in 680, settled in what is now Bulgaria. That led to a number of wars with the Byzantines.

Many other battles ensued over the succeeding centuries. One of the most important came in 1071, when a group of Muslims known as Seljuk Turks defeated the Byzantine army at Mazikert. The Seljuk Turks had been threatening the empire's eastern border for many years, without posing any significant threat. In 1071, however, their leader Alp Arslan was able to gather as many as 100,000 troops to invade Byzantium. The Byzantine Emperor, Romanus Diogenes, was relatively new to his role and didn't have the experience or support to counter the attack.

The Turks had crossed into Byzantine territory and taken the fortresses of Akhlat and Manzikert. Romanus Diogenes' army managed to recapture the two fortresses. The Turks counterattacked, and after several hours of fighting the outnumbered Byzantines withdrew, intending to return to camp for the night. The Turks continued to attack the withdrawing

Turks at war

Byzantine army, so Romanus Diogenes gave the order to turn and fight. Unfortunately, one of the emperor's commanders and his forces ignored the order and continued back to camp. This act of treason left the main army an easy target for the Turks. The emperor himself was captured, and the bulk of the Byzantine army was destroyed. The Turks now had control of much of modern-day Turkey. Few battles had such dramatic and long-lasting far-reaching effects.[3] Many historians view the Battle of Manzikert as the moment when the Byzantines lost the war against the Turks.

In 1095, Byzantine emperor Alexios I appealed to Pope Urban II for help in fighting off the encroaching Muslims. Urban granted the request, and called on Christians throughout Europe to regain the Holy Lands and recapture Jerusalem from the Muslims who occupied it. What became known as the First Crusade began the following year and the Crusaders defeated the Turks in two battles in 1097. They continued through Syria and into Palestine where, in 1099, they won back Jerusalem. The reclaimed lands were turned over to the Byzantines and the crusaders set up four nearby crusader states.

Muslim forces eventually began fighting to regain control of their lost land. The attacks resulted in a series of eight more Crusades. One of them, the Fourth Crusade from 1202 to 1204, would have a profound effect on Constantinople and the Byzantine Empire.

General Belisarius

Emperor Justinian's troops were led into some of their most famous battles by a general named Flavius Belisarius.

Belisarius

Born about 500, Belisarius joined the military as a young man. He was working as one of Justinian's bodyguards when he came to the emperor's attention. By the time he was about 25 years old, he was given permission to begin building his own military unit. The unit grew and grew until it became the center around which all of Byzantium's armies would be organized. His soldiers were armed with composite bows, spears, throwing darts, and swords; they were prepared for all types of battle.

Belisarius and his troops re-conquered much of the territory that had been lost by the Western Empire during the previous century, extending the Empire's borders to their fullest extent. Belisarius's many successes made him popular with both his troops and the citizens of Constantinople—a fact that made Justinian jealous. In 548, Justinian forced Belisarius to retire.

Belisarius remained loyal to Justinian. In 559, he was called back to duty to fight off an army of Huns who had invaded Byzantium. Even though he and his small army were victorious, Belisarius was accused of corruption in 562 and put in jail. Justinian pardoned him the following year. Belisarius died in 565.

Despite his disgrace in later years, most historians agree that Belisarius was one of the most effective generals to serve the Byzantine Empire.

Hagia Sophia is an important monument for the Byzantine Empire. The building was first a church (known as the Church of Santa Sophia), later a mosque, and is now a museum.

CHAPTER 4

Byzantine Religion and Culture

In the beginning, Byzantine culture was primarily a continuation of the Roman Empire. Over the centuries, however, Byzantium changed into a very different civilization. The Empire was influenced by settlers from other lands and political threats from other cultures. In the end, the Empire developed a historical and cultural character all its own, based on a mixture of Greek, Roman, European, Persian, and Islamic elements.

Constantinople was Byzantium's cultural center. Most of the Empire's teachers, writers and artists lived and worked within the city.

Education was at the core of Byzantine culture. Not all Byzantine citizens attended school, but most members of the upper and middle classes learned to read and write. Only men were allowed access to higher education. Some women, most notably those from the households of ruling families, continued their learning by reading on their own or studying with private tutors. State-run primary schools were available to teach children in many of the empire's cities and villages. Byzantine schools taught lessons in grammar, literature, philosophy, science, mathematics, and music.

No matter the age of the student, all Byzantine education was based on the beliefs and teachings of the Christian church, most importantly recognizing Jesus of Nazareth as Christ the Savior. The Christian church was central to Byzantine culture with all citizens—from aristocrats to farmers—taking part in frequent, heartfelt religious debates.

Citizens enjoyed reading religious histories and biographies and many made the effort to read and memorize compositions by ancient authors. Virtually no works of fiction existed unless they were stories about saints' lives. Debate about religious subjects was commonplace and the desire to share their beliefs with others was widespread. Even the Byzantines' creative outlets were largely inspired by their faith. Throughout their long history, they used art, architecture, writing, and music to share their love of God.

Because so much importance was placed upon education, teachers were considered important members of society. Classroom teachers and university professors were required to pass the empire's rigorous exams before they could instruct; their salaries were paid by the local or imperial government.[1]

One of the Empire's most notable architectural developments was the dome. When Emperor Justinian I set out to rebuild war-ravaged buildings in the sixth century, he was determined to improve upon what had existed before. His architects came up with a plan to use a dome roof to cover square or rectangular churches, tombs and other buildings. One of the most famous examples of this new style of Byzantine architecture can be seen in the Church of Santa Sophia, an imposing domed building that has withstood well over than 1,000 years of attacks by mankind (wars, fires, riots) and nature (earthquakes). It is regarded as one of the finest examples of Byzantine architecture. Today known as Hagia Sophia, it still stands and is a museum.[2]

Mosaic decoration was another triumph of this society. Mosaics made of tiny glass or marble tiles were often applied to the domes, walls, and floors of Byzantine churches. Artists used plaster and tiles to create puzzle-like portraits, most often of religious figures or scenes.

Still another important product of Byzantium's artistic community was the painting of devotional panels. These individual scenes of religious significance could be displayed alone or with other panels to tell a story.

Hagia Sophia

As time passed, Byzantine art transitioned from being very classical to more symbolic or abstract in nature. Some historians suggest this change came about simply because artists were not as talented; others see it as a natural progression and suggest that Byzantine painters were beginning to draw inspiration from Asian art.

Of course, visual art came in many forms and Byzantine craftsmen were also widely respected for their enamel work, ivory carving, and metalwork. Byzantine silks, which were manufactured by the empire itself, were considered luxury items.

In addition to portraying religious images, Byzantine art was often used to express imperial power. The emperor's image was displayed in sculpture and circulated on coins or commemorative dishes. Emperors used specially designed gold seals to mark their documents and wore robes and belts that were hand-embroidered and bejeweled. Byzantine craftsmen worked with precious metals, enamel, ivory, and crystal to create spectacular jeweled crowns and orbs. They were particularly skilled at carving elephant tusks, pressing coins, and weaving complex, multicolored designs in silk.[3]

Emperor Justinian thought regal adornment was so important that he reissued laws, reminding citizens that only the emperor was allowed to use pearls, emeralds or hyacinths to decorate his horse's saddle or bridle or even his own belt.[4] A similar law made it illegal for anyone except the emperor to wear purple silk.

While the most luxurious fabrics and expensive gems were reserved for the emperor, other high-ranking political advisors wore costumes as well. Gold buckles, intricate copper pins, embroidered emblems, and gold collars helped commoners identify their government's leaders.

A discussion of Byzantine art would be incomplete without mention of its music and dance. While the music itself has not been preserved, written descriptions suggest that it most often consisted of sacred chants and followed religious services or rituals. It is thought that these chants were performed by individuals as well as by choirs and were accompanied by instruments including the pipe organ. In addition to church settings, these musical performances were often included in royal galas, theatrical events, and empire-sponsored celebrations. Although most examples of Byzantine secular music are long gone, historians theorize that music was passed on orally until the eleventh century, when it began to be recorded on paper.[5] The mere act of recording these notations is thought to have encouraged new compositions—either new words to accompany well-known tunes, or new songs altogether.

Dance within the Empire was initially considered educational and dance classes were a part of the school curriculum. However, as Greek culture gradually became more prominent, dancing was thought to be less educational and more designed for entertainment. The Eastern Roman Empire sought to ban dance for being ungodly. However, church leaders ultimately decided it was better to make dance acceptable by refining it and spiritualizing it. The church began promoting dances that featured circles or processions in which men, separated from women, performed slow, formal movements. While details about the era's dances are scarce, some images of Byzantine dancers have been saved in paintings and sculptures.

Iconoclasm

Iconoclasm was the most controversial policy adopted by the Byzantine Empire.

The Empire had a long tradition of producing icons, which were paintings and other artistic images of Jesus

Hagia Sophia Christ

and other religious figures. Many of these icons were considered to be superb works of art. They were regarded as inspirational and encouraged devotion to the figures they depicted.

Byzantine Emperor Leo III decided that the use of icons violated the Bible's Second Commandment: "Thou shall not make unto thee any graven images." He and his supporters decided that many citizens were actually worshipping the icons rather than the figures they represented.

In 726, Leo began the policy of iconoclasm, which literally means "breaking idols." Soldiers were assigned to remove icons from all public and religious buildings. When this happened, the monks were enraged, and riots ensued.

The "First Iconoclasm" lasted from 726 to 787. At that point, Irene—who first served as regent on behalf on her young son Constantine VI and then took power for herself, becoming the first true Byzantine empress—changed the law and restored icons. The Empire's "Second Iconoclasm," called for by Emperor Leo V, occurred from 814 to 842. By 843, Emperor Michael III was able to work with church leaders to end iconoclasm and restore the use of religious images.

With the exception of some woven tapestry icons and some painted icons at the Monastery of St. Catherine on Mount Sinai, Egypt, very few early Byzantine icons survived the Iconoclastic period.

This oil painting, "The Taking of Constantinople," was created by Italian artist Jacopo d'Antonio Negretti, who was also known as Jacopo Palma.

The Final Centuries

The fall of Byzantium is one of the most-discussed, often-debated subjects in world history because the Empire had been so strong and so important for so many centuries. It had a long-lasting influence on trade, education, politics, architecture, and the arts. Its rulers and people also had worked tirelessly to spread Christianity throughout the land.

Throughout the centuries of its existence, the Empire had countless enemies and endured many bloody battles. However, most scholars agree these battles were not what led to its decline. Instead, it is widely thought that poor leadership and a weakened economy—one which eventually could not even afford to support the navy—were to blame for the Byzantine Empire's demise.

Historians have a hard time deciding exactly when things began to fall apart for the Byzantines. More often than not, Emperor Justinian I is blamed for starting the Empire's troubles.

Justinian ruled from 527 to 565, a time period during which the Byzantines were almost always at war. The huge expenses of maintaining an army, along with his ambitious plans to rebuild Constantinople after the Nika Revolt of 532, nearly bankrupted the Empire. Rulers who succeeded Justinian were forced to increase taxes just to keep the empire running.

Stability started to return to the region in the eighth century but it was short-lived because members of the Empire's upper class began to try to steal away farmland controlled by peasant workers. There were ongoing battles as the aristocrats tried to take over the land and enslave the peasants.

Emperor Basil II, who governed from 976 to 1025, is thought to have ruled over as many as 18 million subjects—one million of them in Constantinople.[1] Basil II believed strongly that free peasantry was essential to the Empire's economy. He worked to protect them and lower their taxes. At the same time he raised taxes on church and nobility. They didn't like the situation but could do little to oppose it.

After Basil II's death in 1025, the Byzantine Empire had a series of weak emperors with little military experience. Under their rule, nobles

**Emperor Basil II
with his guards**

did as they pleased and free peasantry declined. This meant that the army, which had relied upon peasant soldiers, had to hire private, foreign troops.

To pay for the new soldiers, the government had to raise taxes, which caused even more peasants to lose their land, which forced the government to hire more foreign soldiers. This cycle weakened the economy so badly that the Byzantines could no longer afford to maintain their navy.

With no navy, the Byzantines were forced to rely on the Italian city-states of Venice and Genoa to fight their battles for them. In exchange for their military protection, Venetians and Genoese were no longer required to pay import fees. This lowered the Byzantines' trade earnings, which meant they had even less money to spend on defense and other services, which meant they had to rely more heavily on the Italians.

At the same time the Byzantine economy was collapsing, the Empire was being threatened by the Seljuk Turks. In 1071, the Turks defeated the imperial army at Manzikert, claiming part of the Balkans and most of Asia Minor, and capturing Emperor Romanus Diogenes.

As the twelfth century began, swarms of western Europeans moved into the Byzantine Empire. They came to fight the Turks and stayed to find their fortunes. Unfortunately, ongoing conflicts between these European immigrants and the Byzantines put the Empire on the road toward destruction.

By 1200, the Byzantine Empire was just a skeleton of its former self. The Byzantine army was the weakest it had been in centuries. Emperors, who by this time had very little power, temporarily managed to keep Constantinople safe by making deals with the Ottomans, a new group of Turks who had come out of Asia. In 1204, Crusaders from Western Europe who had originally intended to conquer Jerusalem, instead invaded and conquered Constantinople. The crusaders set buildings on fire and destroyed buildings, statues and paintings. Many ancient Greek and Roman manuscripts were lost in the attack, but copies of some of the classics were recovered and eventually taken to libraries in Italy and Muslim Spain.[2]

This map of Constantinople dates back to 1422 and is the oldest surviving map of the city.

When the Crusaders formed what they called the Latin Empire in the ruins of Constantinople, many of the city's citizens fled to the Empire of Nicaea in Asia Minor. There, the refugees established a Byzantine government in exile. The Nicaean Empire declared war on the Latin Empire in 1211 but neither side scored a clear victory.

Then, in 1261, Emperor Michael VIII and the Byzantine army invaded and recaptured Constantinople. Michael VIII and his successors were not as triumphant in their attempts to reconquer other parts of the empire. By the beginning of the fourteenth century, the empire was low on resources and its land claims were limited to Constantinople and small parcels in Asia Minor and the Balkans.[3]

In 1453, Ottoman leader Mehmet II set his sights on Constantinople. Byzantine Emperor Constantine XI mounted a defense centered around a makeshift army of 8,000 men, who battled gallantly against the Ottomans' 100,000 soldiers. After more than a month, the Ottomans got enough soldiers over Constantinople's walls to take the city. Thousands of Byzantine soldiers and citizens were killed in the attack, including Constantine. The victorious Ottomans made the city the new capital of their empire. Eventually they renamed it Istanbul, the name by which it is still known today.

The Byzantine Empire had finally fallen, but its effects on art, education, politics and religion would live on for generations to come.

Blues vs. Greens

Noted comedian Rodney Dangerfield once said that "I went to a fight the other night and a hockey game broke out."

Chariot race

While it's true that modern-day hockey, football, soccer, and even baseball fans have been known to go overboard in terms of supporting their teams, they have nothing on the fans of Byzantine-era chariot racing fans.

Chariot racing was the most popular form of entertainment in Constantinople. Fans of the Empire's two most popular teams, the "Blues" and the "Greens," would crowd into the 80,000-seat Constantinople Hippodrome to cheer on their favorite racers. Chariot racing was so popular that these rival groups even managed to affect politics. Looking more like fierce gangs than sports fans, they often shouted out demands to the emperor after a big win. When they weren't cheering at chariot races or functioning as unofficial political parties, members of the Blues and the Greens engaged in fights that occasionally resulted in murders.

The Blues vs. Greens feud climaxed in 532, when the Nika Riots broke out after the government tried to punish members of the groups for a series of killings that happened after an important chariot race.

In an odd twist, the Blues and Greens briefly joined forces, setting the city on fire and attempting to overthrow the emperor. Emperor Justinian—a longtime supporter of the Blues—offered a bribe to the Blues' leaders. No longer united in their assault on the government, the Blues abandoned the Greens, leaving nearly 30,000 of them to be killed by the imperial army.

Ancient Craft: Medallion

The Byzantine Empire used pendants and medallions to classify residents according to social status, religion and political office. In 529 AD, Emperor Justinian proclaimed that only members of the noble class were allowed to wear sapphires, emeralds, and pearls, while other precious stones could be worn by any social class.

You can make your own Byzantine-inspired medallion. Your finished medallion can be hung with a ribbon or string.

MATERIALS
- Air-dry clay
- Colorful rhinestones
- Staining and antiquing medium
- Assorted acrylic craft paints
- Small paintbrushes
- Water-based polyurethane varnish
- Wooden rolling pin
- 12x12-inch square of canvas or waxed paper
- Round cookie cutters or plastic drinking cups
- Clay tool set (or you can improvise with assorted household tools)

DIRECTIONS
1. Form a clay ball the size of a golf ball. Place the ball on canvas or waxed paper and flatten with your hand. Use the wooden rolling pin to continue to flatten clay until it is about one-fourth of an inch thick.
2. Using the cookie cutter or plastic drinking cup, cut a circle out of your flattened clay. Consider making medallions in a variety of sizes. Use your fingers to smooth edges.

3. Use clay tools, kitchen utensils, screwdrivers and other household items to create patterns. Press rhinestones into the clay. If you plan to hang your medallion, incorporate a hanging hole in the design, leaving at least one-fourth of an inch of clay around it.

4. Allow the medallion to harden. Carefully pick it up and rotate it on the canvas or waxed paper (this will help it dry gradually and evenly). It will take about 48 hours for your medallion to cure completely.

5. When your medallion is dry, it's time to stain it. Mix acrylic paint with the staining and antiquing medium, according to package instructions. You can apply colors with your fingertips or a small brush.

6. When the stain is dry, seal the medallion with a non-toxic, water-based acrylic polyurethane varnish. Apply two coats for indoor display or four coats for outdoor display. Be sure to apply the varnish to the back of the medallion as well as the front.

7. Display the medallion on a shelf or hang with a ribbon or string.

Ancient Recipe: Pastfeli

The birth of the Byzantine Empire introduced new spices, sugar, and vegetables to cooks who were working to merge Greek and Roman recipes. The Byzantines were adventurous eaters. Some of the most popular meals included seafood, lamb, bread, cheeses, citrus fruits, salad, and eggplant. While very few cookbooks from this time period exist, historians believe Byzantines had a particular fondness for sweet treats and drinks.

This candy would provide a sweet ending to a Byzantine meal. Make certain you ask an adult for assistance when using the stove.

INGREDIENTS
½ cup honey
½ cup sesame seeds
1 tsp. orange flower water

DIRECTIONS
1. Place honey in a heavy sauce pan. Using a candy thermometer, heat the honey to 250 to 256 degrees Fahrenheit. This is known as "firm ball" stage; at this stage, the honey will form thick threads as it drips from the spoon. If you dropped a little of this honey into cold water it would form a hard ball that, with pressure, you could flatten. Don't guess about the temperature. Use a candy thermometer!
2. Stir in the sesame seeds and continue cooking until the mixture comes to a boil.

3. Spread the mixture half an inch thick on a tray moistened with orange flower water. Orange flower water is also known as orange blossom water. It is distilled from bitter orange blossoms and used to flavor drinks, salads and desserts. You'll find it in many specialty food stores.

4. Allow to cool completely, then cut into small diamonds or squares.

330	Roman Emperor Constantine I rebuilds the ancient Greek city of Byzantium, makes it the capital of the Roman Empire, and it is named for him.
364	Roman Emperor Valentinian I divides the empire into western and eastern sections. Valens is the first emperor of the Eastern Empire.
476	The Western Empire falls. The Eastern Empire survives and becomes known as the Byzantine Empire.
527	Justinian I's reign begins. He is supported by his wife, Empress Theodora.
554	The Byzantine Empire reaches its peak in terms of size and power.
602	Emperor Maurice is overthrown. Persia attacks the empire and makes claims to large territories of land.
610	Heraclius becomes emperor. The Empire's language changes to Greek.
626	Constantinople is attacked by both Avars and the Persians. The city survives as both enemy forces withdraw.
634-37	Arab Muslims conquer Syria, followed by their conquest of Jerusalem.
680	The Bulgars establish a kingdom within the Balkans.
693	Muslims attack Constantinople.
717-18	Emperor Leo III successfully defends Constantinople against an attack by the Muslim army and navy.
726	Emperor Leo III bans the use of icons.
811	The Bulgars kill Emperor Nicephorus I in battle.
843	The use of icons is restored.

924	The Bulgars unsuccessfully attack Constantinople.
976	Basil II becomes Emperor.
992	The Venetians are granted trading rights in the Byzantine Empire.
995-96	Emperor Basil II retakes Syria from the Muslims and Greece from the Bulgars.
1054	The western and eastern branches of the Christian Church permanently separate.
1071	The Turks defeat the Byzantine army at Manzikert, claiming part of the Balkans and most of Asia Minor, and capture Emperor Diogenes Romanos.
1096	Crusaders arrive at Constantinople. The Crusaders are successful in their goal of capturing Jerusalem three years later, but eventually end their alliance with the Byzantines.
1171	Emperor Manuel I withdraws Venice's trading privileges within the empire.
1204-5	The Fourth Crusade captures Constantinople and establishes the Latin Empire of Constantinople. Emperor Theodore Lascaris sets up Nicaea, a Byzantine government in exile.
1261	Nicaea's army recaptures Constantinople and restores the Byzantine Empire.
1449	Constantine XI becomes the last Byzantine emperor.
1453	The Ottoman Turks capture Constantinople, killing Constantine XI. The Byzantine Empire comes to an end.

Chapter Notes

Chapter 1 Birth of an Empire

1. Judith Herrin, *Byzantium*: *The Surprising Life of a Medieval Empire* (Princeton, New Jersey: Princeton University Press, 2007), p. 7.
2. Ibid., pp. 5-6.
3. Cyril A. Mango, *The Oxford History of Byzantium* (Oxford, England: Oxford University Press, 2002), p. 69.
4. James A. Corrick, *World History Series*: *The Byzantine Empire* (San Diego, California: Lucent Books, 1997), p. 18.
5. Comer Plummer III, "Ancient History: Walls of Constantinople." *Military History,* June 12, 2006.
   www.historynet.com/ancient-history-walls-of-constantinople.htm.

Chapter 2 A Complex Machine

1. James A. Corrick, *World History Series*: *The Byzantine Empire* (San Diego, California: Lucent Books, 1997), p. 24.
2. Ibid., p. 28.
3. "Theodora (Byzantine Empress)." *Encyclopedia Britannica Online.*
   www.britannica.com/EBchecked/topic/590611/Theodora.
4. Judith Herrin, Byzantium: *The Surprising Life of a Medieval Empire* (Princeton, New Jersey: Princeton University Press, 2007), pp.150-151.
5. Cyril A. Mango, *The Oxford History of Byzantium* (Oxford, England: Oxford University Press, 2002), p. 144.
6. "Byzantium and the West (Getty Exhibitions)." The J. Paul Getty Museum.
   http://www.getty.edu/art/exhibitions/byzantium

Chapter 3 Battles, Battles Everywhere

1. Warren Treadgold, *A Concise History of Byzantium* (New York: Palgrave, 2001), pp. 71-72.
2. James A. Corrick, *World History Series*: *The Byzantine Empire* (San Diego, California: Lucent Books, 1997), p. 71.
3. J. Rickard. (15 October 2000), *Battle of Manzikert,* 19 August 1071.
http://www.historyofwar.org/articles/battles_manzikert.html

Chapter 4 Byzantine Religion and Culture

1. James A. Corrick, *World History Series*: *The Byzantine Empire* (San Diego, California: Lucent Books, 1997), p. 49.
2. Warren Treadgold, *A Concise History of Byzantium* (New York: Palgrave, 2001), p. 84.
3. Judith Herrin, *Byzantium*: *The Surprising Life of a Medieval Empire* (Princeton, New Jersey: Princeton University Press, 2007), p. 52.
4. Cyril A. Mango, *The Oxford History of Byzantium* (Oxford England: Oxford University Press, 2002), p. 60.
5. Herrin, *Byzantium,* p. 227.

Works Consulted

Chapter 5 The Final Centuries

1. Dr. Kenneth W. Harl, "Early Medieval and Byzantine Civilization: Constantine to Crusades." Tulane University, March 19, 1998. http://www.tulane.edu/~august/H303/handouts/Population.htm

2. James A. Corrick, *World History Series: The Byzantine* Empire (San Diego, California: Lucent Books, 1997), pp. 94-55.

3. Ibid., p. 97.

Works Consulted

Angold, Michael. *Byzantium: The Bridge from Antiquity to the Middle Ages.* New York: St. Martin's Press, 2001.

Arnott, Peter. *The Byzantines and Their World.* New York: St. Martin's Press, 1973.

"Byzantium and the West (Getty Exhibitions)." The J. Paul Getty Museum. http://www.getty.edu/art/exhibitions/byzantium

"Byzantium: Byzantine Studies On The Internet," Fordham University. www.fordham.edu/halsall/byzantium

Corrick, James A. *World History Series: The Byzantine Empire.* San Diego, California: Lucent Books, 1997.

Harl, Dr. Kenneth W. "Early Medieval and Byzantine Civilization: Constantine to Crusades." Tulane University, March 19, 1998. http://www.tulane.edu/~august/H303/handouts/Population.htm

Harris, Jonathon. *Byzantium and the Crusades.* London: Hambledon and London, 2003.

Herrin, Judith. *Byzantium: The Surprising Life of a Medieval Empire.* Princeton, New Jersey: Princeton University Press, 2007.

Mango, Cyril A. *The Oxford History of Byzantium.* Oxford, England: Oxford University Press, 2002.

Plummer, Comer III. *"Ancient History: Walls of Constantinople."* Military History, June 12, 2006. www.historynet.com/ancient-history-walls-of-constantinople.htm.

Rickard, J. (15 October 2000), *Battle of Manzikert,* 19 August 1071. http://www.historyofwar.org/articles/battles_manzikert.html

"Theodora (Byzantine Empress)." *Encyclopedia Britannica Online.* Encyclopedia Britannica. www.britannica.com/EBchecked/topic/590611/Theodora.

Treadgold, Warren. *A Concise History of Byzantium.* New York: Palgrave, 2001.

Books

Adams, Simon and Katherine Baxter. *The Kingfisher Atlas of the Ancient World.* New York: Kingfisher Publishing, 2006.

Bingham, Jane and Sam Taplin. *Encyclopedia of the Ancient World.* London, England: Usborne Books, 2007.

Dubois, Muriel L. *Ancient Rome: A Mighty Empire.* North Mankato, Minnesota: Capstone Press, 2011.

Halstead, Rachel. *Hands-on History Projects: Home Life: Learn About Houses, Homes and What People Ate in the Past, with 30 Easy-to-Make Projects and Recipes.* Leicester, England: Anness Publishing, 2009.

Vanvoorst, Jennifer Fretland. *The Byzantine Empire (Exploring the Ancient World.).* North Mankato, Minnesota: Compass Point Books, 2012.

On the Internet

The Byzantine Empire – World History for Kids
    http://www.kidspast.com/world-history/0142-byzantine-empire.php

Byzantine Art – Encyclopedia Britannica online
    http://www.britannica.com/EBchecked/topic/87136/Byzantine-art

Encyclopedia of Food & Culture via Enotes
    http://www.enotes.com/byzantine-empire-reference/byzantine-empire

Justinian – Byzantine History for Kids
    http://www.historyforkids.org/learn/medieval/history/byzantine/justinian.htm

Kids History: Byzantine Empire
    http://www.ducksters.com/history/middle_ages_byzantine_empire.php

HowStuffWorks: Byzantine Empire
    http://history.howstuffworks.com/european-history/byzantine-empire.htm

Glossary

archaeologist (ahr-kee-AWL-uh-jist) – a person who specializes in the scientific study of prehistoric people and their cultures by analyzing their artifacts

barbarians (bar-BEAR-ee-ons) – people considered as uncivilized, cruel or warlike. In the days of the Byzantine Empire, this term was specifically used to refer to members of tribal societies that tried to invade it

dynasty (DIE-nuh-stee) – a succession of rulers from the same family

etiquette (EHT-uh-keht) – rules governing the proper way to behave

excavation (eks-kuk-VAY-shuhn) – the process of uncovering artifacts by digging away at the earth

extravagance (ik-STRA-vuh-gens) – very showy and expensive

hierarchy (HIE-uhr-ohr-key) – persons or things ranged in ranks or classes

hippodrome (HIP-uh-drom) – large open-air stadium with an oval course for horse and chariot races

incompetent (in-KOM-puh-tent) – lacking skills or intelligence

looted (LOOT-ed) – pillaged or stolen, especially in time of war or unrest

negotiation (ni-go-she-A-shun) – discussions held to reach an agreement or settlement

nomadic (no-MAD-ik) – wandering from place to place with no permanent home

obelisk (AW-buh-lisk) – a tall, four-sided, narrow tapering monument which ends in a pyramid-like shape at the top

peninsula (puh-NIN-suh-luh) – a piece of land that projects into a body of water and is connected to a larger landmass

revolt (ree-VOLT) – to rise up against a government or its ruler

secular (SEK-yoo-luhr) – not godly

spiritualizing (spear-uh-choo-LIES-ing) – giving a spiritual meaning to something

Index